the
BIG BOOK

Taylor Swift

by Bianca Burnett

© Burnett Books 2023

Table of Contents

Part 1: Early Years & Country Roots

Part 2: Rise to Stardom

Part 3: Musical Evolution: Transition to Pop

Part 4: Global Fame: Staying Authentic

Part 5: Big Reputation: Legacies and Achievements

Part 6: Beginning Again: Future Directions

Early Years & Country Roots

Taylor Alison Swift was born on December 13, 1989 in Reading, Pennsylvania. Raised in a close-knit family, Taylor displayed an early affinity for music. Her parents recognized her passion and encouraged her pursuits, laying the foundation for a future superstar. By elementary school, Taylor was already expressing her creativity through songwriting, a talent that would shape her remarkable career. Swift's family played a crucial role in fostering her artistic endeavors, supporting her aspirations to become a country music singer.

Taylor Fact #1

Taylor received her first guitar at the age of 10 as a Christmas gift, sparking her interest in learning to play and driving the start of her musical career.

Early Years & Country Roots

Taylor's childhood was marked by a love for storytelling. She found joy in the works of artists like Shania Twain and developed a keen interest in the country music genre. These early influences would later weave into the fabric of her songwriting, contributing to the unique narrative style that sets her apart. Swift's childhood was a time of exploration and self-discovery, as she honed her musical skills and learned to play various instruments. It was during this formative period that she began performing at local events and contests, showcasing the budding talent that would eventually capture the world's attention.

Taylor Fact #2

Taylor's grandmother, Marjorie, was a professional opera singer. It was her grandmother's legacy that encouraged her passion for singing and performing.

Early Years & Country Roots

Taylor's family relocated to Nashville when she was 14, a pivotal move that allowed her to immerse herself in the heart of the country music scene. Nashville, often referred to as the "Music City," provided the perfect backdrop for Swift's ambitions to flourish. Swift's determination was evident as she tirelessly performed at local venues, talent shows, and open mic nights.

Swiftie Survey

What Is Taylor's favorite childhood book?

Answer on the next page!

Early Years & Country Roots

Swift's breakthrough came in 2004 when she showcased her talent at the Bluebird Cafe, a legendary Nashville venue. Scott Borchetta, a music executive, happened to be in the audience and recognized her star potential. Impressed by her stage presence and the emotional depth of her songs, Borchetta approached Swift and offered her a record deal with his newly formed label, Big Machine Records.

Swiftie Survey

Answer: To Kill a Mockingbird by Harper Lee

Taylor Fact #3

Taylor wrote her first original song, "Lucky You," at the age of 12.

Did you know?

Taylor's brother Austin Is 2 years younger than her. Despite Taylor's global fame, the siblings maintain a private and supportive relationship

At 14 years old, Taylor Swift was the youngest songwriter ever hired by Sony/ATV.

Her lucky charm is a necklace with a gold number 13 pendant.

Swift's first movie role was in the 2009 film "Valentine's Day."

Andrea (Taylor's mom) wanted to name her daughter Taylor because she didn't people to be able to know her gender just by reading her name.

Rise to Stardom

Released when she was just 16, her first album "Taylor Swift" not only showcased her songwriting prowess but also established her as a rising star in country music. Hits like "Tim McGraw" and "Teardrops on My Guitar" resonated with audiences, and Swift's relatable lyrics and genuine charm endeared her to fans worldwide. The success of her debut marked the beginning of a meteoric rise, earning her critical acclaim and recognition within the industry.

Swiftie Survey

What is one of Taylor's favorite foods?

Answer on the next page!

Rise to Stardom

The album showcased her innate ability to tell stories through music, capturing the highs and lows of adolescence and the nuances of teenage love. With her signature curls and a guitar in hand, Taylor Swift quickly endeared herself to audiences, not just for her musical prowess but also for her relatability, becoming a role model for young fans. Little did she know that her authentic storytelling would catapult her into superstardom, making Taylor Swift a household name and influencing a generation of music lovers worldwide.

Swiftie Survey

Answer:
Cheeseburgers!

Quotes

"People haven't always been there for me, but music always has."

"If you're lucky enough to be different, don't ever change."

"I'm intimidated by the fear of being average."

—Taylor

Rise to Stardom

From 2006 to 2009, Taylor shared her debut album with fans while opening for several popular Country artists Including Rascal Flatts, Kenny Chesney, and Tim McGraw. The album achieved considerable commercial success, reaching the fifth position on the Billboard 200 chart in the United States. It secured the top spot on the Top Country Albums Chart for twenty-four non-consecutive weeks and earned a quadruple platinum certification from the Recording Industry Association of America (RIAA). This was the longest time for an album on the billboard 200 chart in the last decade!

Swiftie Survey

How many Grammy Awards has Taylor received?

Rise to Stardom

Taylor Swift's process of writing her "Fearless" album was a deeply personal and introspective journey that reflected her experiences and emotions during a crucial period in her life. Released in 2008 when she was just 18, the album showcased Taylor's growth as a songwriter. Taylor stated about writing "Fearless": "I've written a lot of songs by myself lately, especially since I've been alone so much on the road," she said. "I do love writing on the road – I usually write at the concert venue. I'll find a quiet place in some room at the venue, like the locker room."

Swiftie Survey

12 Grammys (and is the first woman to win album of the year 3 times!)

Did you know?

Taylor has a collection of vintage Polaroid cameras – one of which she used to shoot her "1989" album cover.

Taylor has a charitable foundation called the Taylor Swift Education Center.

Taylor is known for her love of baking and often shares her creations on social media. Check out her chai sugar cookie recipe!

Taylor has a tattoo of the number 13 on her hand.

Taylor debuted a line of fragrances, including "Wonderstruck" and "Taylor."

Rise to Stardom

As she began to piece together the album, the title came to her while writing one of the lead tracks. To Taylor, "fearless doesn't mean you're completely unafraid and it doesn't mean that you're bulletproof. It means that you have a lot of fears, but you jump anyway." The "Fearless" album marked a pivotal moment in Swift's career, not only because of its commercial success but also showcased her writing on a larger stage. Securing its debut at No. 1 in the United States, the album went on to dominate as the best-selling album of 2009, with an impressive sales figure surpassing 3.2 million copies. At the mere age of 18, Taylor Swift earned the distinction of becoming the youngest artist in history to boast the year's top-selling album. To champion the album, Taylor Swift started off on her first concert tour, spanning from 2009 to 2010.

Quotes

"You are not the opinion of someone who doesn't know you."

"I never want to change so much that people can't recognize me."

"You can't have a better tomorrow if you're thinking about yesterday all the time."

—Taylor

Taylor Fact #4

On May 18, 2022, Taylor Swift was bestowed with an honorary Doctor of Fine Arts degree from New York University and assumed the role of commencement speaker for the ceremony.

Taylor Fact #5

While Taylor Swift usually writes using her given name, she adopted the pseudonym "Nils Sjöberg" while writing the song "This Is What You Came For," a collaboration with Calvin Harris featuring Rihanna.

Taylor Fact #6

Taylor can play more than just guitar – she is also proficient in playing the piano, banjo, and ukulele!

Musical Evolution: Transition to Pop

Taylor Swift's transition to pop music marked a pivotal moment in her career, signaling a bold departure from her country roots. This change began to emerge in her third album "Speak Now". She continued to exhibit her signature confessional style but also demonstrated a musical maturation that blends elements of country, pop, and rock. Notably, Swift wrote every song on the album entirely by herself, showcasing her lyrical prowess and unique ability to capture the nuances of her own experiences. The album's title, "Speak Now," is a directive, urging the listener to speak up in the moment, a sentiment echoed throughout the tracks.

Swiftie Survey

How tall Is Taylor?

Musical Evolution: Transition to Pop

Songs like "Mine," "Back to December," and "Enchanted" navigate themes of love, heartbreak, and self-discovery. Beyond its musical richness, "Speak Now" is remarkable for its narrative continuity. Each song functions as a chapter in a larger story, weaving together a tapestry of emotions and reflections. In support of "Speak Now", Swift took her captivating storytelling from the studio to the stage. Her worldwide tour was characterized by its commitment to fan engagement. Swift often incorporated surprise elements into her shows, inviting fans on stage, responding to signs in the audience, and creating a sense of camaraderie that transcended the typical concert experience.

Swiftie Survey

5 foot 10 inches

Did you know?

Taylor Swift is a supporter of the Blank Space Fund, which aids education programs in New York City.

Taylor has been named Billboard Magazine's 'Woman of the Year' twice.

Taylor Swift played the guitar and sang the national anthem at a Philadelphia 76ers game when she was 11.

She has a wax figure at the Grevin Museum in Paris.

Taylor is an avid fan of crime shows and mystery novels.

Musical Evolution: Transition to Pop

Swift continued to venture into the pop scene in creation of her next album: "Red". It was a sonic exploration for Swift, who collaborated with a diverse group of producers and songwriters, including Max Martin and Gary Lightbody. The album is notable for its genre-bending approach, incorporating elements of pop, rock, and even dubstep. As she navigated the complexities of love and loss, Taylor Swift's "Red" not only resonated with fans but also established her as a versatile artist capable of transcending genres and capturing the intricacies of the human experience. Taylor channeled her feelings into a diverse set of tracks that ranged from upbeat anthems like "We Are Never Ever Getting Back Together" to poignant ballads like "All Too Well."

Musical Evolution: Transition to Pop

"Red," Taylor Swift's fourth studio album released in 2012, catapulted to immense commercial success, solidifying her status as a global pop phenomenon. The album quickly achieved multi-platinum status, selling over 1.2 million copies in its first week in the United States alone. "Red" received critical acclaim for its diversity in sound and solidified her status as a powerhouse in the music industry. Swift states, "All these emotions — spanning from intense love, intense frustration, jealousy, confusion, all of that — in my mind, all those emotions are red."

Swiftie Survey

What is Taylor Swift's longest song title?

Musical Evolution: Transition to Pop

Taylor Swift's "Red" World Tour, launched in support of her critically acclaimed fourth studio album, took the globe by storm from 2013 to 2014. The tour was a spectacular visual and musical extravaganza, reflecting the dynamic range of emotions encapsulated in the album. The concerts were characterized by elaborate stage setups, stunning visuals, and Swift's signature intimate interactions with the audience. The setlist featured a mix of fan-favorites from the "Red" album, including hits like "I Knew You Were Trouble" and "22," alongside energetic renditions of her earlier classics.

Swiftie Survey

"We Are Never Ever Getting Back Together"

Quick Quiz

Which of Taylor's Musical Genres are you?

What's Your Ideal Weekend Activity?
a) Horseback riding in the countryside
b) Hitting the hottest clubs and dancing
c) Attending a live rock concert

Favorite Lyrics Style?
a) Storytelling and narrative-driven
b) Catchy and relatable
c) Edgy and rebellious

Your Go-To Instrument?
a) Acoustic guitar
b) Synthesizer/Keyboard
c) Electric guitar or drums

Fashion Choice for a Night Out?
a) Cowboy boots and denim
b) Trendy and fashionable outfits
c) Leather jackets and band t-shirts

Favorite Movie Genre?
a) Western or small-town drama
b) Romantic comedy
c) Fast-paced action movie

Quick Quiz

Which of Taylor's Musical Genres are you?

Mostly A's:
Country Enthusiast

As a certified Country Enthusiast, your penchant for cowboy boots, acoustic strums, and the simple joys of rural life align perfectly with the soulful twang of country melodies.

Your vibrant energy, love for catchy beats, and affinity for the latest trends make you the life of the musical party, where every pop anthem is your personal soundtrack.

Mostly B's:
Pop Aficionado

Mostly C's:
Rock Rebel

Your passion for edgy riffs, rebellious anthems, and the electric energy of live performances makes you a true rock lover.

Quotes

"I've always been fascinated by the idea that a song can be there forever."

"Anytime someone tells me that I can't do something, I want to do it more."

"I think the perfection of love is that it's not perfect."

-Taylor

Taylor Fact #7

Taylor's very first acting appearance was on "C.S.I.: Crime Scene Investigation" in 2009!

Did you know?
Cats Edition

Taylor Swift's love for cats is well-known, and her feline companions have become an integral part of her public persona.

Taylor has two Scottish Folds named Meredith Grey and Olivia Benson, as well as a Ragdoll named Benjamin Button.

The cats have even made cameo appearances in Taylor's music videos, adding a playful and personal touch to her creative projects.

Taylor adopted Benjamin Button after meeting him on the set of her "Me!" music video.

Taylor takes her cats anywhere and everywhere with her - often in custom-made cat carriers or lounging in plush accommodations.

Musical Evolution: Transition to Pop

Taylor Swift's definitive transition from country to pop occurred during the production of her "1989" album, released in 2014. This switch is what many consider marks a defining moment in her career. Embracing a vibrant pop sound with influences from the 1980s, Swift worked with renowned pop producers such as Max Martin and Shellback to craft a collection of infectious and synth-driven tracks. Hits like "Shake It Off" and "Blank Space" demonstrated her ability to seamlessly adapt to the pop genre, earning her critical acclaim and a broader fan base. Taylor noted, "The inspiration behind this record, I was listening to a lot of late 80s pop ... I really loved the chances they were taking, how bold it was. It was apparently a time of limitless potential, the idea you could do what you want be what you want ... the idea of endless possibility was kind of a theme in the last two years of my life."

Musical Evolution: Transition to Pop

The accompanying "1989 World Tour" further solidified Taylor Swift's metamorphosis into a pop sensation. The tour, which spanned from 2015 to 2016, was a dazzling spectacle filled with elaborate stage setups, dazzling visuals, and costume changes. Swift envisioned a tour that would not only bring her new sound to life but also redefine the concert experience.

Collaborating with a team of top-tier professionals, including renowned director Baz Luhrmann and choreographer Tyce Diorio, Taylor meticulously designed every aspect of the tour. The result was a visually stunning and highly choreographed production that featured elaborate stage setups, mesmerizing visuals, and a series of thematic segments reflecting the diverse influences of the "1989" album.

Swiftie Survey

What is the name of Taylor Swift's documentary released on Netflix in 2020?

Musical Evolution: Transition to Pop

This transition was not only evident in her music but also reflected in her public persona, as she confidently embraced a more contemporary and sophisticated image. Beyond her musical endeavors, 2014 was a year of personal growth for Taylor Swift. Her highly publicized friendships with fellow celebrities, often referred to as her "squad," gained immense attention, showcasing a supportive network of women in the entertainment industry. Additionally, Taylor continued to assert herself as a savvy businesswoman, advocating for fair compensation for artists in the digital age. As she delved into the pop genre and expanded her influence beyond music, Taylor Swift's life in 2014 demonstrated her ability to adapt, innovate, and maintain her relevance in the ever-changing landscape of the entertainment industry.

Swiftie Survey

"Miss Americana"

Quick Quiz

Which Taylor Swift Album are you?

What's your go-to emotion when dealing with relationships?

A. Nostalgic and reflective.
B. Excited and carefree.
C. Thoughtful and contemplative.
D. Intense and passionate.

Which activity appeals to you the most?

A. Writing in a journal or composing poetry.
B. Dancing and enjoying upbeat music.
C. Playing an instrument or engaging in artistic endeavors.
D. Exploring the great outdoors or trying something adventurous.

Your friends would describe you as:

A. Thoughtful and introspective.
B. Energetic and outgoing.
C. Artistic and sincere.
D. Passionate and adventurous.

Quick Quiz

Which Taylor Swift Album are you?

Pick a setting for a perfect day:
A. An intimate gathering with close friends.
B. A lively music festival with friends.
C. quiet, cozy cafe with a good book.
D. An adventurous day exploring nature or a new city.

How would you describe your ideal Friday night?
A. Cozy night in with a good book or movie.
B. Hitting the town with friends, ready for a night of fun.
C. Attending a low-key gathering with close friends.
D. Exploring a new adventure or outdoor activity.

Pick a color that resonates with you the most:
A. Soft pastels.
B. Bold and vibrant colors.
C. Earthy tones.
D. Rich and deep hues.

Quick Quiz

Which Taylor Swift Album are you?

Mostly A's: "Fearless"

You're most like Taylor Swift's "Fearless" album — sincere, reflective, and ready to embrace the sweet nostalgia that defines the chapters of your love story.

You're most like Taylor Swift's "1989" album — fun, carefree, and destined to dance through life with vibrant energy and a touch of unpredictability.

Mostly B's: "1989"

You're most like Taylor Swift's "Speak Now" album — a genuine soul, embracing heartfelt moments and personal connections.

Mostly C's: "Speak Now"

You're the "Red" album — intense, passionate, and ready to embrace the diverse emotions that make every love story a captivating journey.

Mostly D's: "Red"

38

Taylor Fact #8

Taylor Swift's "Fearless" album not only won Album of the Year at the 2010 Grammy Awards but also made her the youngest artist to ever win that category at the age of 20.

Taylor Fact #9

During high school, Taylor Swift was known as a social butterfly and even won the title of her high school's mascot, the Eagle, in a school-wide vote.

Taylor Fact #10

In 2019, an asteroid was officially named 327796 Taylorswift in honor of the singer's contributions to music and philanthropy.

Taylor Fact #11

In 2013, Taylor Swift received a Golden Globe nomination for Best Original Song for "Safe & Sound," which she co-wrote for the film "The Hunger Games."

Quotes

"Happiness and confidence are the prettiest things you can wear, and I hope you wear them often."

"I've come to the realization that it's ridiculous to be afraid of anything in life because most of the things we're afraid of never happen."

"Change is never easy, you fight to hold on, and you fight to let go."

-Taylor

Global Fame & Staying Authentic

Swift has never shied away from sharing her joys, heartbreaks, and self-discoveries in her songwriting. From the innocent tales of young love in her early country albums to the more complex narratives in her pop era, she invites listeners into her world, creating a genuine connection that transcends the boundaries of fame. This openness fosters a sense of relatability, making her not just a global superstar but someone audiences feel they know intimately. Taylor Swift's authenticity lies in her unapologetic advocacy for herself and others. From standing up for fair compensation for artists against streaming services to using her platform to speak out against inequality, Swift has consistently demonstrated a commitment to her principles. Her bold move to address issues directly, whether in her music or in public statements, showcases a refusal to conform to industry norms or public expectations.

Global Fame & Staying Authentic

Despite the authenticity admired by her fans, Taylor Swift's career journey has not been immune to controversy. Taylor Swift notably retreated from the public eye, marking a departure from her usual engagement with fans and the media. One of the primary catalysts for this decision was the intense scrutiny and public backlash she faced during a fued with Kanye West. Swift became embroiled in controversy after snippets of a phone call between Swift and Kanye West were released, challenging the narrative Swift had maintained about her involvement in West's song "Famous." The resulting public scrutiny and accusations of dishonesty seemed to take a toll on Swift's mental and emotional well-being. Faced with an overwhelming wave of negativity, Swift chose to step back and reassess her approach to fame, opting for a period of relative seclusion.

Global Fame & Staying Authentic

This era was marked by Swift's desire to reclaim control over her narrative. Facing a barrage of media speculation and sensationalism throughout her career, she decided to go on a strategic hiatus, allowing the public narrative to fade away while she worked on her next move. This period of "going dark" was characterized by her absence from social media and public appearances, creating a shroud of mystery around her actions. Ultimately, this deliberate withdrawal allowed Swift the space to reinvent herself creatively and emerge with the Reputation album, which not only addressed the controversies head-on but also showcased her ability to transform personal challenges into artistic triumphs.

Swiftie Survey

Which music streaming service did Taylor Swift temporarily remove her music from in 2014?

Global Fame & Staying Authentic

In November 2017, Taylor Swift finally unveiled Reputation, her sixth studio album. Taylor writes in the prologue of her "Reputation" album, "Let me say it again, louder for those in the back...We think we know someone, but the truth is that we only know the version of them that they have chosen to show us." The record marked a departure from her previous work, embracing a darker and more electronic sound that incorporated elements of synth-pop and R&B. The lyrics delved into themes of reputation, public perception, and the personal toll of fame.

Swiftie Survey

Spotify

Did you know?

In 2013, Swift danced with Prince William at the Winter Whites Gala in Kensington Palace. The duo danced to the hit song "Livin' on a Prayer" by Bon Jovi.

Taylor popularized the term "Swiftmas" to describe her habit of surprising fans with personalized gifts, especially during the holiday season.

For each album, Taylor creates a set of personal journals filled with thoughts, song lyrics, and experiences related to that specific chapter of her life.

Swift has a unique fear - sea urchins. She once mentioned in an interview that they are her biggest phobia.

While Taylor is naturally right-handed, she taught herself to write with her left hand.

Taylor Fact #12

Taylor often practices her songs on a treadmill to build stamina for her energetic stage performances.

Taylor Fact #13

While Taylor Swift initially kept her political views private, she broke her silence in 2018 and endorsed Democratic candidates in the midterm elections.

Taylor Fact #14

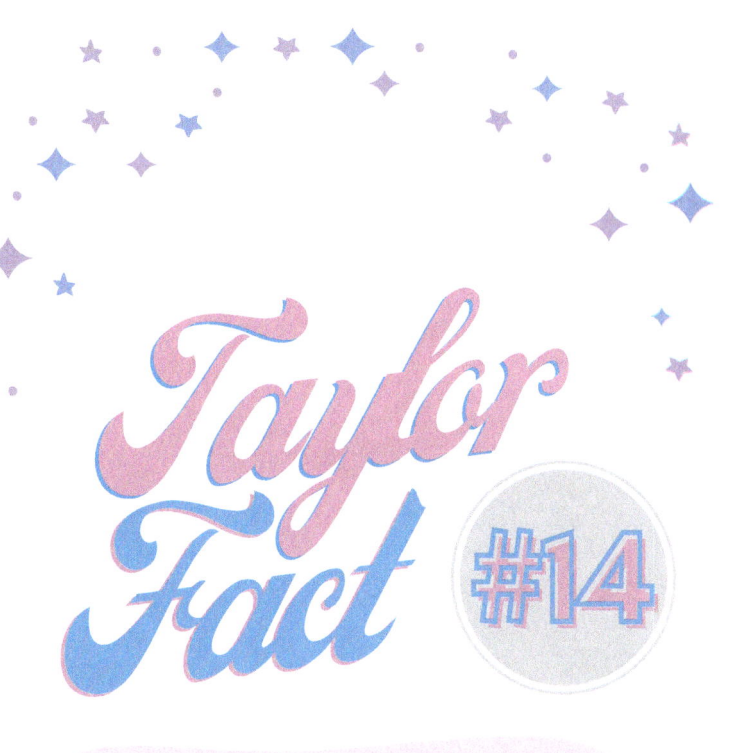

Taylor Swift's love for historic homes led her to purchase a property in Rhode Island known as "the Harkness House".

Taylor Fact #15

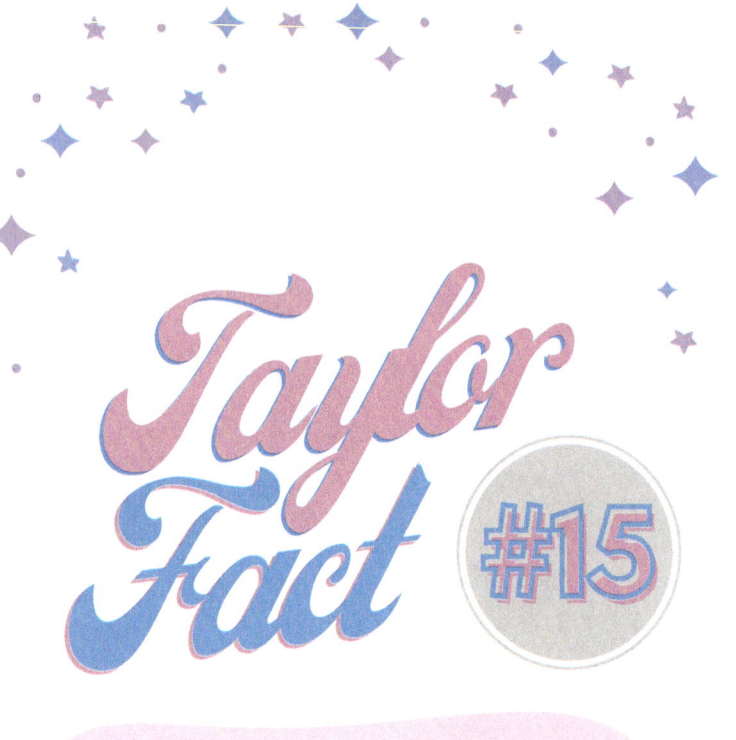

Taylor Swift's childhood nickname was "Tater Tot," given to her by her family.

Global Fame & Staying Authentic

Tracks like "Look What You Made Me Do" and "...Ready for It?" hinted at a more assertive and unapologetic Taylor, confronting the controversies and criticisms she had faced. The album also showcased her ability to blend genres, experimenting with production styles that were a departure from her country and pop roots. Swift's Reputation era was not just a musical evolution but a strategic reclamation of her narrative, turning the negative spotlight into a powerful artistic statement.

Reputation became an instant commercial success, topping charts worldwide and solidifying Taylor Swift's status as a resilient force in the music industry.

Global Fame & Staying Authentic

The Reputation Tour, launched in 2018, was a meticulously designed spectacle that showcased Taylor Swift's resilience and marked a significant departure from her previous concert productions. The tour was conceptualized to complement the themes of her Reputation album, which delved into issues of public perception and personal growth. The stage design incorporated innovative elements, including a massive, high-tech video screen that spanned the length of the stadium. The production also featured a snake motif, referencing the symbol that had been used against her during a public feud and emphasizing her ability to transform adversity into empowerment. The success of the Reputation Tour was nothing short of phenomenal. With over 2 million tickets sold and a gross revenue exceeding $345 million, it became one of the highest-grossing concert tours of all time.

Global Fame & Staying Authentic

Taylor Swift's life took a more private turn when she met British actor Joe Alwyn. The two began dating in 2016, and their relationship marked a departure from Swift's previous high-profile romances. Keen on keeping their love out of the public eye, Swift and Alwyn maintained a low-key relationship, with limited appearances together in the media. The influence of Joe Alwyn on Taylor Swift's life became palpable in her seventh studio album, "Lover," released in 2019. Departing from the darker tones of her previous album "Reputation," "Lover" embraced a more optimistic and romantic theme. The title track, "Lover," offered a glimpse into Swift's relationship with Alwyn, featuring heartfelt lyrics that celebrated the simplicity and enduring nature of true love.

Quotes

"Being strong is not about having a brave face; it's about having a brave heart and staying true to yourself."

"In my mind, you should be proud of your mistakes."

"You have people come into your life shockingly and surprisingly."

—Taylor

Taylor Fact #16

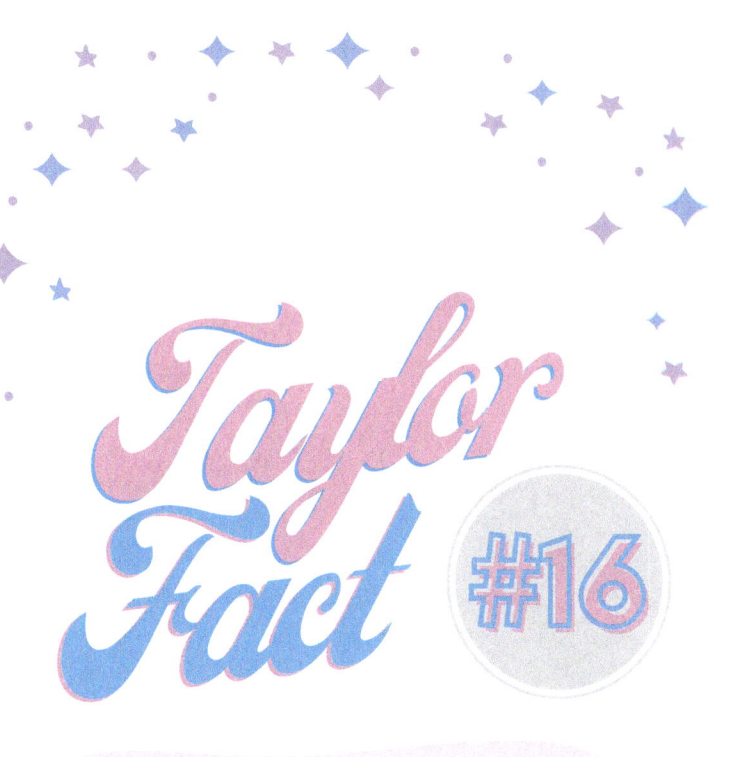

Swift had a cameo appearance in "Hannah Montana: The Movie" (2009). She played herself in a humorous scene where she mistakes Miley Cyrus's character for a gardener.

Taylor Fact #17

Taylor Swift is listed as a co-inventor on two U.S. patents involving a stage setup that allows performers to interact with fans in the audience through a rotating or elevating platform.

Taylor Fact #18

Swift grew up on a Christmas tree farm in Pennsylvania. The experience inspired her holiday hit, "Christmas Tree Farm," released in 2019.

Global Fame & Staying Authentic

The idea for her tour "Lover Fest" emerged as a celebration of her seventh studio album, "Lover," which was known for its romantic and uplifting themes. The tour was designed to capture the essence of the album. The stage was expected to be a vibrant and dreamlike setting, adorned with colorful aesthetics, reminiscent of the album's artwork. However, when the COVID-19 pandemic swept across the globe, the unprecedented health crisis led to the cancellation of events worldwide, including "Lover Fest". Despite the disappointment, Swift demonstrated resilience and understanding, emphasizing the importance of solidarity during these challenging times. While Lover Fest couldn't proceed as planned, Taylor Swift continued to engage with her fans through alternative means, such as virtual performances and surprise releases.

Taylor Fact #19

In 2015, Taylor wrote an open letter to Apple Music, criticizing their decision not to pay artists during the free trial period for users, leading Apple to change their policy.

Taylor Fact #20

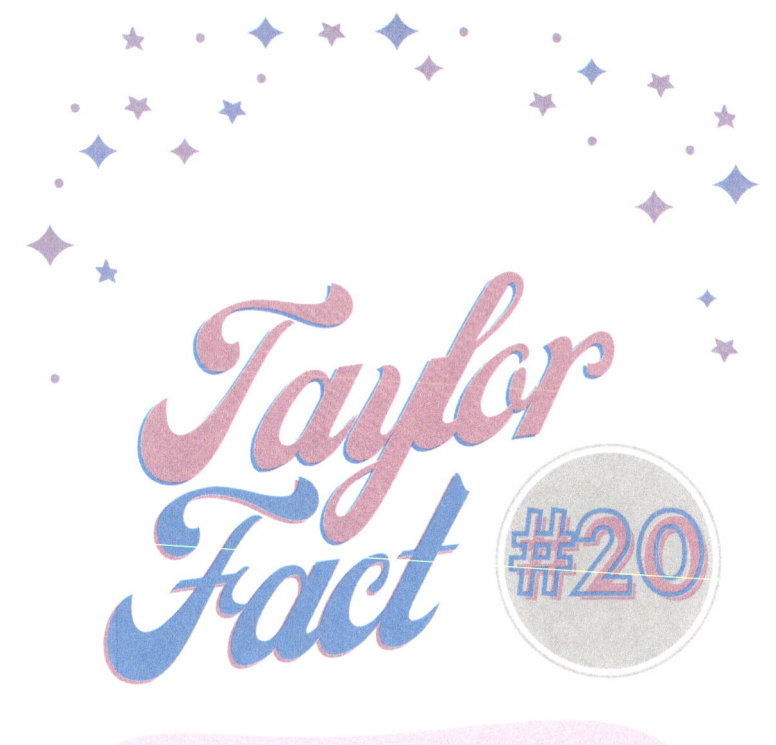

Taylor Swift grew up as a fan of the football team the Philadelphia Eagles.

Taylor Fact #21

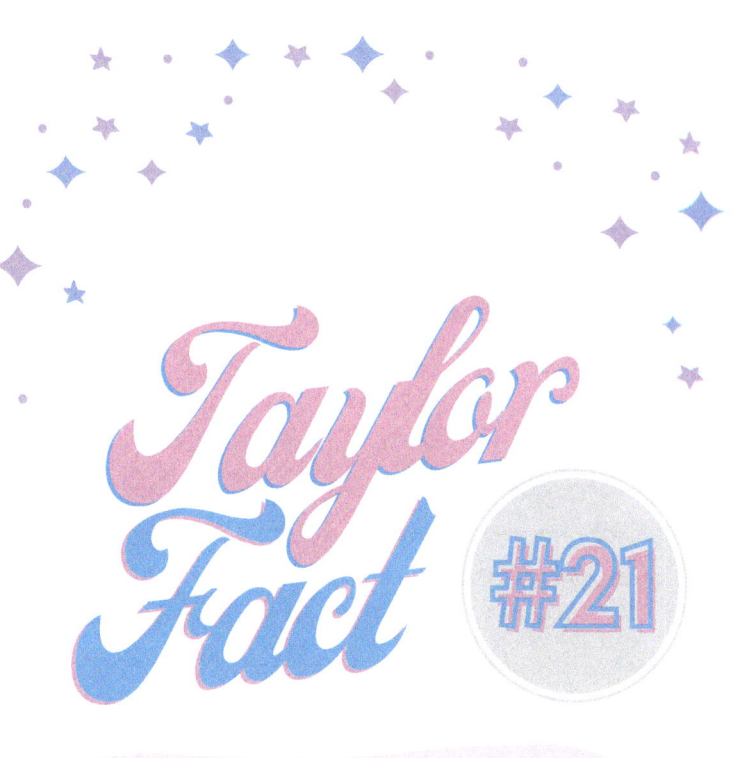

Taylor Swift used the pseudonym Paul McCartney when checking into hotels to maintain privacy.

Big Reputation: Legacies & Achievements

Secluded from the world, Swift harnessed the solitude to craft two surprise albums, "Folklore" and "Evermore." Departing from the polished pop sounds that had characterized her previous work, these albums marked a significant shift toward indie folk and alternative rock. The writing process was a clandestine endeavor, with Swift collaborating remotely with Aaron Dessner of The National, Jack Antonoff, and other key contributors. The albums' introspective and melancholic themes reflected the uncertainty of the times, mirroring the collective global experience of isolation and introspection during the pandemic.

Swiftie Survey

To pass the time on set, what does Taylor like to do?

Big Reputation: Legacies & Achievements

Swift's decision to surprise-release both "Folklore" in July 2020 and "Evermore" in December 2020 was a strategic departure from the traditional album release cycle. By opting for an unannounced drop, she embraced spontaneity and direct connection with her audience. The surprise release strategy not only generated immense excitement among fans but also allowed Swift to share her creative process more authentically. Swift's ability to adapt to the unique circumstances of the pandemic, channeling the isolation into a burst of creativity, demonstrated her resilience as an artist and solidified her reputation as a trailblazer in the ever-evolving landscape of the music industry.

Swiftie Survey

Crossword puzzles!

Big Reputation: Legacies & Achievements

A crucial element defining Taylor Swift's legacy is her strategic move to re-record her albums, reclaiming ownership and control over her musical catalog. The saga surrounding the sale of Taylor Swift's master recordings began in 2019 when her former label, Big Machine Label Group, was acquired by music executive Scooter Braun's company, Ithaca Holdings. This acquisition included the rights to Taylor Swift's first six albums, a move that Swift vehemently opposed. The situation intensified as Swift claimed she was not given the opportunity to buy her masters before the sale. Swift's reaction was candid and emotional, expressing her disappointment and sense of betrayal. This event sparked a larger conversation within the music industry about artists' rights to own their master recordings.

Taylor Fact #22

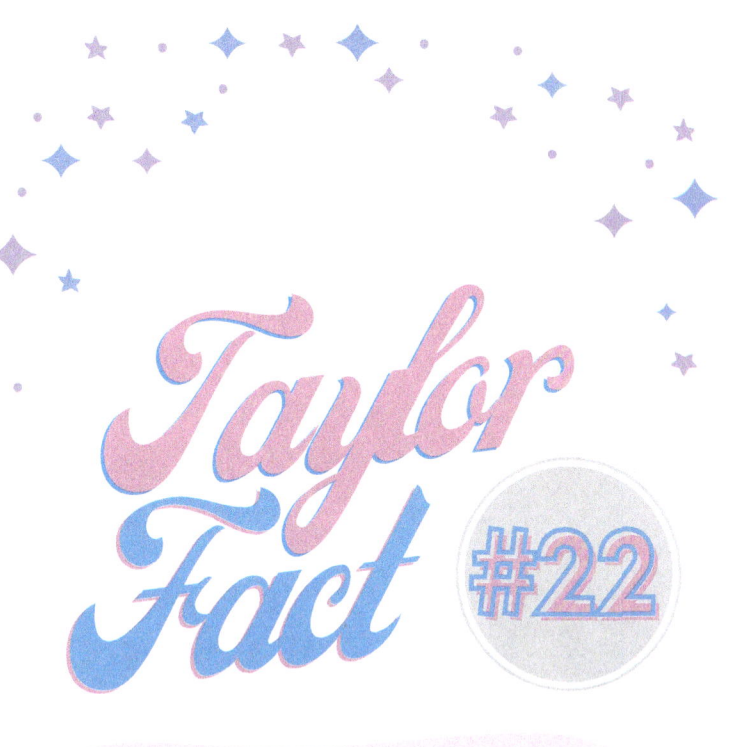

Taylor Swift and Selena Gomez share a close friendship. They met when they were both dating Jonas Brothers (Swift with Joe Jonas and Gomez with Nick Jonas) and have remained friends since then.

Taylor Fact #23

Swift has expressed her interest in detective work and has mentioned that if she wasn't a musician, she might have pursued a career as a detective.

Taylor Fact #24

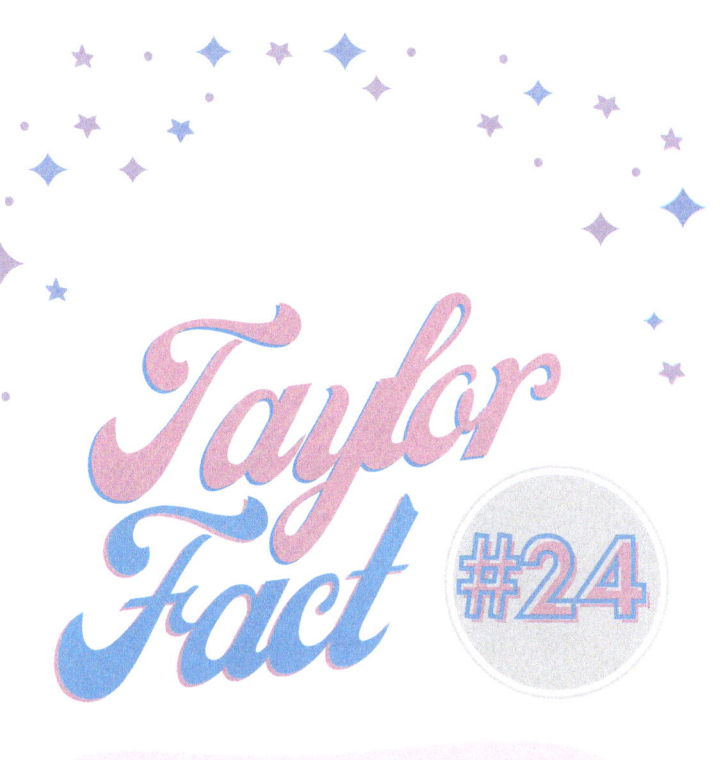

Swift's habit of embedding hidden messages in her album booklets became widely known, but during her early career, she would capitalize certain letters to spell out secret messages.

Big Reputation: Legacies & Achievements

In response to the loss of her masters, Taylor Swift devised a bold plan to regain control over her discography. She announced her intention to re-record her early albums, starting with "Fearless," which was released in 2021 as "Fearless (Taylor's Version)." By re-recording her albums, Swift aimed to create new master recordings that she would own and control. This strategic move not only allowed her to reclaim her artistic work but also served as a form of empowerment in the face of a challenging industry landscape. The re-recordings also became a way for Swift to engage with her loyal fanbase and provide them with fresh interpretations of the beloved classics. This decision also sparked an important conversation about artists' rights and the dynamics of ownership in the music industry.

Big Reputation: Legacies & Achievements

The release of "Red (Taylor's Version)" marked a significant chapter in Taylor Swift's journey to reclaim control over her master recordings. This highly anticipated album, a re-recording of her 2012 original "Red," became a testament to Swift's resilience and determination in the face of industry challenges. Following this re-release, Swift also went on to release "Speak Now (Taylor's Version)" and "1989 (Taylor's Version)". With each release, Swift not only revisits the cherished songs from her past but also unveils previously unreleased tracks "from the vault", offering fans a treasure trove of fresh material. These vault tracks provide a unique insight into Swift's creative process during the original recording sessions, granting listeners a glimpse into the artistic decisions that shaped the albums.

Quick Quiz

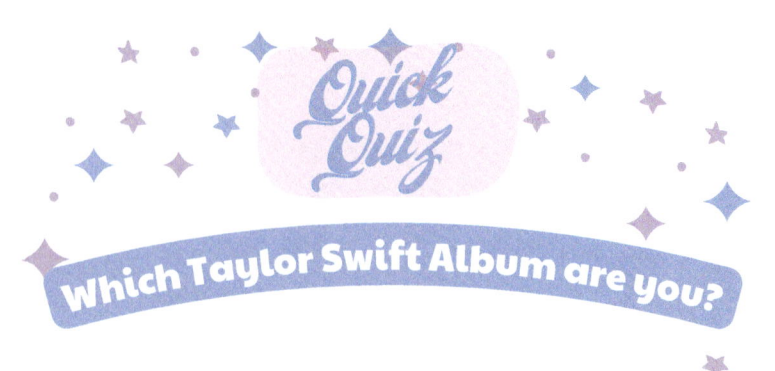

Which Taylor Swift Album are you?

Pick a word that resonates with you the most:
A. Enchanting
B. Whimsical
C. Bold

What's your preferred musical vibe?
A. Folk and indie sounds with a touch of mystique.
B. Mellow and introspective tunes
C. Edgy and dynamic tracks that pump up the energy.

How do you handle challenges or setbacks?
A. Reflecting on the deeper meaning in solitude.
B. Navigating through emotions & seeking solace in creativity.
C. Confronting issues head-on and embracing resilience with a bold attitude.

Quick Quiz

Which Taylor Swift Album are you?

Your friends would describe you as:
- A. Dreamy and introspective.
- B. Thoughtful and empathetic.
- C. Confident and adventurous.

What color palette resonates with you the most?
- A. Earthy tones and deep blues.
- B. Soft pastels and muted hues.
- C. Bold reds and dark, dramatic colors.

Choose an ideal setting for a night out:
- A. A forested glade with a bonfire and stargazing.
- B. A quaint coffee shop with acoustic live music.
- C. A lively club with a pulsating dance floor.

Quick Quiz

Which Taylor Swift Album are you?

Mostly A's: "Evermore"

Your serene and enchanting spirit aligns perfectly with the magical essence of Taylor Swift's "Evermore" album

Embrace the gentle melodies and thoughtful introspection – your affinity whimsy aligns beautifully with Taylor Swift's enchanting "Folklore" album.

Mostly B's: "Folklore"

Mostly C's: "Reputation"

Your bold and confident spirit resonates powerfully with the dynamic energy of Taylor Swift's "Reputation" album, reflecting your fearless approach to life.

Taylor Fact #25

Taylor Swift's favorite holiday movie is reported to be "Love Actually".

Taylor Fact #26

Swift has a tradition of placing emotionally poignant songs as the fifth track on her albums.

Taylor Fact #27

Taylor Swift is a big fan of ice cream. In fact, her favorite flavor is reportedly Mint Chocolate Chip.

Big Reputation: Legacies & Achievements
By the Numbers

12 Grammy Awards

40 American Music Awards

29 Billboard Music Awards

23 MTV Music Awards

Big Reputation: Legacies & Achievements

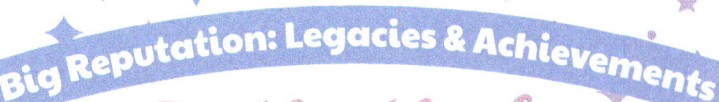

By the Numbers

8 — Academy of Country Music Awards

12 — Country Music Association Awards

2 — Brit Awards

1 — Emmy Award

Big Reputation: Legacies & Achievements
Records Broken

Youngest Album of the Year Winner: Taylor Swift became the youngest artist to win the Grammy Award for Album of the Year for her album "Fearless" in 2010.

First Female Artist to Win Album of the Year Twice: Swift won the Grammy for Album of the Year twice, making her the first female artist to achieve this feat.

First Solo Female Artist to Win the CMA Entertainer of the Year Twice: Swift won the Country Music Association (CMA) Award for Entertainer of the Year twice, becoming the first solo female artist to do so.

Big Reputation: Legacies & Achievements
Records Broken

Most Billboard Music Award Wins in a Single Year by a Female Artist: Swift set a record for the most wins by a female artist in a single year at the Billboard Music Awards in 2015.

Most Top 10 Debuts in Billboard Hot 100: Swift holds the record for the most Top 10 debuts on the Billboard Hot 100.

Fastest-Selling Digital Album: "Red" (2012) became the fastest-selling digital album by a female artist.

Big Reputation: Legacies & Achievements
Records Broken

First Artist to Debut at No. 1 on the Billboard Hot 100 and Billboard 200 Simultaneously:
Swift achieved this feat with "Cardigan" and "Folklore," respectively.

Most Spotify Streams in a 24-Hour Period:
Swift's song "Look What You Made Me Do" set a record for the most streams in a single day on Spotify.

Fastest-Selling Album in Over a Decade:
"Red (Taylor's Version)" set records for the fastest-selling album in over a decade within its first day of release.

Beginning Again: Future Directions

Taylor has already achieved an unfathomable amount of success In her career. Taylor Swift has consistently demonstrated versatility and innovation in her approach to music, continuously surprising fans and the industry with her creative endeavors. Taylor's most recent release outside of her re-recordings was her album "Midnights". Swift writes of this new album, "This is a collection of music written in the middle of the night, a journey through terrors and sweet dreams." At the 2023 MTV Video Music Awards, Swift secured nine victories, notably clinching Video of the Year for "Anti-Hero," a remarkable achievement as it marked her fourth win in this category. Additionally, she garnered six nominations at the 66th Annual Grammy Awards, achieving a historic seventh nomination for Song of the Year with "Anti-Hero."

Taylor Fact #28

Taylor Swift and Ed Sheeran developed a secret handshake during their friendship, which they once performed on the red carpet together.

Taylor Fact #29

Taylor Swift is an avid horse lover and has been riding since she was a child.

Taylor Fact #30

Swift is known for her love of Christmas, and she even has an annual Christmas tradition of making snow globes for her friends.

Quotes

"I think the tiniest little thing can change the course of your day, which can change the course of your year, which can change who you are."

"Never be afraid to stand up for yourself; sometimes you have to be your own hero."

"Perfect is boring, and human is beautiful."

—Taylor

Beginning Again: Future Directions

After the triumph of "Midnights," Taylor eagerly anticipated reconnecting with her fans in person post the COVID-19 pandemic. This desire for interaction with her audience sparked the concept of "The Eras Tour." The tour was crafted to encompass songs from all of Taylor's previous musical eras while also commemorating the new ones that were yet to be experienced in a live setting. March 2023 started "the Eras Tour", a spectacle that garnered widespread attention from media for its significant cultural and economic influence. The U.S. segment of the tour achieved a groundbreaking feat by breaking the record for the highest number of tickets sold in a single day. Ultimately, the Eras Tour emerged as Taylor Swift's most extensive touring endeavor, encompassing 62 shows in the U.S. and 89 shows internationally, totaling an impressive 151 shows worldwide.

Beginning Again: Future Directions

Anticipating Taylor Swift's future directions in her career is a dynamic endeavor, as she has consistently surprised audiences by transcending musical genres and experimenting with new sounds. Looking ahead, one could envision her continuing to explore diverse musical landscapes, possibly delving into collaborative projects that further showcase her adaptability. Given her outspoken advocacy for artists' rights and social issues, it's conceivable that she will continue leveraging her platform to champion causes close to her heart. As a consummate artist and trailblazer, Taylor Swift's future endeavors are likely to be marked by continual reinvention, leaving an indelible impact on both the music industry and the broader cultural landscape.

the BIG BOOK OF Taylor Swift

Printed in Great Britain
by Amazon